Love from the Yellowstone Trail

Love from the Yellowstone Trail

Sharon Chmielarz

NORTH STAR PRESS OF ST. CLOUD, INC.
St. Cloud, Minnesota

ISBN 978-0-87839-687-0

First Edition, June 2013

Published in the United States of America

Cover by: Benjamin Pratt (Midwest Artist)
E-mail: BPratt976@msn.com.
Painting photographed by: Doug Burg
Author photo by: Mark Cryderman

Published by
North Star Press of St. Cloud, Inc.
P.O. Box 451
St. Cloud, Minnesota 56302

www.northstarpress.com   Facebook - North Star Press   Twitter - North Star Press

Dedication

For the Johnnies and Piuses, Alberts and Josephs,
Turning Hearts and Walking Elks, Charlies,
Mables, Dorothys and Marys
the Chicago, Milwaukee, St. Paul and Pacific
carried off over the river to wars and sometimes returned.

Table of Contents

First a River

> "All of it happened slow . . ."
> —Stanley Kunitz

First a River, the Missouri 3
First Baptist Church, Variations on Water 5
Fire and Water 6
The Preacher on Daniel and Ezekiel 8
Three on Water 9
The River's Arguments 11
River Woman 12
A Voice Shines Upon You 13

Notes from the Trail

> "It was beginning winter. The light moved slowly over the
> frozen field."
> —Theodore Roethke

Notes from the Trail 17
"10th November, Satturday 1804" 21
Love from the Yellowstone Trail 22
Two Voices from the Trail 24
Finding Sacajawea 25
Braiding Three Reports to Make One Fact 26
Wounded Knee 27
Dance Site on Standing Rock 28
Borders 29
The Wind 30
Another Love Letter 31
Haying 32
The Genealogist's Table 33
Cream Puffs 34
Old Glory Passes By 35

Houses

"We went from house to wood. For change in solitude."
—Robert Frost

About Houses 41
How Do We Live in Winter Without Zinnias? 44
Six Meditations on French Doors During a War 45
Three on Hell 48
Dress Shoes 49
Bees 50
Teleportation 51
Fixing Potato Salad While the Past Comes and Goes 52
Of the Little Store near the Park, the Best 53
Spider Webs 54
Ring 55
The Pillow Cleaners Come to Town 56
Bed 57
West River Wedding 58
The Wedding Feast 59
The Old Made New 60
Two Sisters at the Breakfast Table 61
Like a Train Going By 62

First a River

"All of it happened slow . . ."
—Stanley Kunitz

First a River, the Missouri

1.

Glow of worn velvet. The West.
At twelve I wrote my name and age in its closet.
I knew its hills like friends,
how they change blue-yellow-green,
sentinels keeping time. I knew
dust in hair, shadows in a living room,
tragedies boxed and covered up, a warped
sense of possession. I knew how
in evening it cooled off—
some rest on the forehead,
some grace in quietness,
some darkness coming over its shoulder.
I've seen the river's plain table and its gifts
from the dead daughter, shells, birds,
the white tail which makes its way
through blonde grasses to drink at the shore.

2.

These mountains, too large to be called home.
You run from them for shelter in a town.
You dominate your life, your house, with kitsch.
As for the river, it's more modest,
it stays and it leaves.

Who can compare it to generations?
Made from a forked design—
the Madison, Jefferson, Gallatin—
its bed, brown as a trout or bullhead,
its water, green and blue. Jump two feet
and you've made it from bank to shore.

3.

Pebbles and dirt underfoot. Juniper
musk carried on a chill, May wind.
Here and there, coves along the river,
the charred remains of an evening fire.
Impossible not to want to light one,
if the creature you are is human,
if it's night, and there's driftwood
at hand, and you're with friends
or alone and you're listening
to the river, pocked with age, still
flowing indelibly by.

First Baptist Church, Variations on Water

It rains on paper and salvation when someone leaves
Bibles stacked on the sill and the window open.

The baptistery is our watery altar. Near the pulpit
Virginia Baum leads us on the organ over the waves.

Each voice, its own priest, each note rolling
from the River Jordan and spouting God's blessings.

The lights over the vanquished pews are crowns,
illuminating the gospel from the Sea of Galilee.

On the upper floor, in sleepy classrooms,
stories run like rivers through Jerusalem's alleys.

Jesus, the sweet drop of water in the desert.
Jesus, the living water from the Nazarene's well.

We are rowing in the pink brick church
off the Yellowstone Trail bordering North Main.

We are rowing, but it gets harder; nowadays
the second floor is boarded off with sheet rock.

A wall to save on fuel. A door in case of emergency.
The preacher's day job is teaching high school.

We are rowing past last Sunday's catastrophe,
the collection's drought, eight dollars and a quarter.

When the Communion tray comes clinking down the pew,
we lift a thimble glass of grape juice and drink in remembrance.

Fire and Water

This year the grass is so dry, a whisper
could set it off. Drought has descended

like summer snow, bleaching the grasslands
along the river, where, for a thousand seasons,

Mandans set the prairie on fire, loosed
the blistering monster to thunder over lives

of the slow-legged and gorge on grass.
Firefighters now, they rush in for a kill, aiming

for the carmine throat. They return home,
soot-faced, hands stuffed with money to burn.

*

We've penned her in, fattened her up, tamed her.
Named her 'reservoir.' All the cottonwoods

on her banks fall, choked with water.
Like corpses they topple, barkless, leafless,

covering themselves with the sadness
of water. Snakes, the harmless but ghastly

bull snakes, slither for cover.
A ghost scene. Scavengers drive out from town,

haul driftwood home, dowel it out
for trays, bowls, candle holders.

*

Citizens meet in the Wrangler, their arms folded
across their chests. They've been double-crossed

by the Corps of Engineers. The Brigadier General
has some explaining to do. They accuse him

of mismanaging the river, allowing in drought
too much water to leave her upper basin.

It flows downstream to fatten people's pockets
two states south. That isn't why farmers agreed

to give up the river for a dam.—It's come to this,
hot air and piss. No one goes home satisfied.

*

She has a marina on the east, Jed's Landing.
Little cabins, cute cabins, you can rent.

Last year Lakotas bought the landing.
But what can they do now for a river's ghost?

Who would recognize her, slim and flowing,
her waves, oh,oh,oh,oh in places. She lies low,

looking at the sky, reflecting the blue
with deep bends. Never overflowing.

In the land's ravines, desire drums
the wet fervor of the former lover.

*

Thundercloud the rancher shows his neighbor,
Joe Keller, a pyre where his Lakota mother

wizens under sun, the body in her slow return
to dust. Keller remembers "dust to dust"

from his own catechism, engrained
in a man with ten children. To him, we're all

Zachariah's shepherds on a thin shore, waving
our dried-up arms, railing at small currents

from large disappointments, excited and fearful
when fire ignites the basin of an ancient sea.

7

The Preacher on Daniel and Ezekiel

Ezekiel, touched forever by visions of griffons and woe,
shouts "Repent, whores, you who pay your lovers! Woe!"

He prefers a diet of beans and lentils, millet and fitches,
barley cakes baked over cow's dung, the smell of woe.

He scatters his hair to the winds. He burns it in protest.
Lamentation upon lamentation. No one listens to his woe.

He won't go up to Temple, where the scum of the country's
abomination hasn't been drained. Shame and woe!

He retreats behind his gates and courts, measured
in cubits, built with not six or five but seven steps of woe.

He's been living back to back with Daniel for ages,
though never beloved like Daniel who interpreted woe.

Daniel the dreamer, bright in science, gifted in language,
reared on the King's meat and Babylon's finest wine and woe.

The furnace Daniel 's cast into is seven times hotter than usual,
per Nebuchadnezzar's command: Burn Daniel, that Prince of Woe.

Daniel walks out alive though not unscarred. Who wouldn't be,
after surviving an inferno, lions' maws, and escaping to tell that woe?

Not a hair singed on his head, yet his heart is clawed by fear,
fear for the next dreamer, the earthly borders to come, the unlimited woe.

Three on Water

1.

Fragrance of rain on wood, a rare moment
in a land where dust rises at the least
provocation in the road before the house.
In the yard, an addition 's going up,
a stack of lumber waits on the sidewalk,
enough for two more rooms, bedrooms
for the six people inside,
locked in sleep, slumbering
through an overnight rain, a gentle
soaker each sleeper registers in dreams.
Between rain and drying, only breathing.

2.

In the baptistery, that small,
red-draped theater
in the church sanctuary,
you're immersed
in salvation and the wavering
light from candle sconces
flanking the choir.
You rise on the preacher's arm,
sputtering like wet fire;
your white robe, soaked.
Your soul cleansed and ready
to join the saved before the Throne.
It stands in lonely myrtle;
doves gray as ash rest on its arms.

3.

Half the town used to drink
railroad water, river water.
You poured a glass from the tap,
and after it had cleared,
you drank slowly,
knowing intimately
as you swallowed,
all that follows, silt
from the past, settles.

The River's Arguments

The river, its arguments smudged
like a wallet from greasy fingerprints,
gives up over its course all carding,
IDs, unions, obituaries, places
and names, business passed by,
or through,
for the greater happiness
of memory—being
somewhere in time, a role
played out and measured
on flood poles. Year-marked. Especially
in small towns levels are noticed,
in cafes where a river runs by windows
and buries fields in silt every century.
Another, muddy world. A fortune in water.
Had the river a license, it'd declare blue
to brown eyes, silver hair on sunny days,
height in miles, weight in tons. Born:
Ought ought ought ought. Old
when the century was young. Old
when the century was old. A member
on Earth whose accent laps over
and under all immigrants'. A member
in good standing with the sky.

River Woman

What her hands need is routine and dust
Turned into flair, the reign of a big spender, perfect
Innuendos found and bought at auctions
And gardens. A little dawn mixed in.
A little embedded evening. The word
Tender, meaning superior, rubbed often.

What her nose needs is a washed and ironed smell,
An early-in-the-week-scent breathing, "That's done."
Names she can snort at, fragrance which is lilacy,
A whiff from the bread basket's tinny, yeasty odor.
A whiff of the Butternut steaming on the counter.
The power of salami lying thick on homemade bread.

What her heart needs is a package of goods.
Things she can see with her hands, fuss
That is small and wiry and can be labeled.
At the back screen door, summer shadow and a wisp
Of cool air floating in. A hungry man on the steps. "Mam."
His blessing for the sandwich before he hops the train.

A Voice Shines Upon You

Someone is singing.
It sounds like a mother.
It sounds like a mother
sending her daughter
off to war
or marriage.
Someone is singing like a mother.

She thinks she just walked out, the refrain goes,
she thinks she just walked out on her own
without any help. She thinks
she did it all on her own.

Someone is singing
lyrics taken from favorable
zodiac readings and charms.
O sea of reeds, o salt sea,
o first born, o wilderness
and inheritance, o fate
with the balled-up fist.

Someone is singing.
It sounds like a mother.
It sounds like an old mother
sending her daughter off
to war
or marriage.
Someone is singing, wavering
like a mother.

Notes from the Trail

It was beginning winter. The light moved slowly over the
frozen field."
—Theodore Roethke

Notes from the Trail

1.

"9th of <u>October</u>, 1804
a windey rainey night, and cold,
So much So we Could not speek
with the Indians to day . . ." (Captain William Clark)

Clark's mechanics reminds me of my father's,
whose journals I found, scrolled, eight
in a tube, a record on butcher paper:

"Oct. 1981 on the 9th
after snowing 4 inchs
a morning dove sang her song"

2.

"<u>February</u> 13th, 1805
I returned last Night from a hunting party
much fatigued, haveing walked 30 miles
on the ice and through Points of wood land
in which the Snow was nearly Knee Deep" (Clark)

Snow was always Knee Deep,
swept into corners, until the first
hint of good weather. Then came song:
walking to the door, throwing it open.

"Feb. 1984 20th
I saw wild geese fly over the Oahe lake
in a straight line and about close to a 1/4th of a mile long,
they were headed north."

"9th of <u>March</u>, 1805
a Cloudy Cold and windey morning wind from the North.
I walked up to See the Party that is makeing Perogues,
about 5 miles above this, the wind hard and Cold.
I wind to the upper mandan Village
& Smoked a pipe with the Chief and returned . . ." (Clark)

For whom does one take notes?
If not for oneself, to prove to someone,
you were here. This grafitti on paper
turns to dust, too; possibly,
your true dust in the universe.

"March, 1980 18th
we went to Kulm today and saw Ducks, medow larks, Crows,
Robins and a gopher . . . north of Eureka we began seeing snow
and when we got to Kulm they had up to 4 feet of the white stuf
and melting, the town is quite flat and water allover. . ."

"9th of <u>April</u>, 1805
I saw a Musquetor to day . . ." (Clark)

When a day turns aimless,
as it can on the Plains' immensity,
horizons incredibly distant,
you can practice setting down
your chair in the exact spot
you picked it up from.

"April, 1985 9th
I did hear a medow lark
across the railroad avenue."

5.

"20th of April, 1805
Saw several buffalow lodged in the drift wood
which had been drouned in the winter . . ." (Clark)

How comfortably death lodges in driftwood,
a small version of the darkness we fear.
The fall from the Garden. Providentially
we land on our own two feet. Wide-eyed.

"April, 1985 4th
Ice on the Oahe . . . is gone, saw a grackle
and short tail black bird on this day . . ."

6.

"19th of April, 1805
the wind so hard from the N.W. that we were fearfull
of ventering our Canoes in the river . . . the Praries appear
to Green, the cotton trees bigin to leave,
Saw some plumb bushes in full bloom . . ." (Clark)

That is the prairie, telling everything
by its appearance, leaving nothing
for the wind but to agree.

"April, 1986 7th
on this day i saw a gopher west of Hosmer,
this was not the striped kind also heard
a medow lark he sounded so good"

7.

"June 13th, 1805
My fare is really sumptuous this evening;
buffaloe's humps, tongues and marrowbones,
fine trout parched meal pepper and salt, and a good appetite;
the last is not considered the least of the luxuries." (Meriwether Lewis)

My father reminded us we ate like kings.
Better. As for him, his mouth always
wanted more, but his stomach said no.
Many times, he disobeyed. It was his
eyes that deceived him;
ah, that bitch of a garden.

"June,1984 11th
Tomatos blooming"

8.

"July 16th, 1805
a fair morning after a verry cold night, heavy dew . . ." (Clark)

You never know when summer will come,
put its feet up on the table, stay awhile,
long enough to know and love the place.

"July, 1985 5th
furnice came on this morning"

"10th November, Satturday 1804"

". . . the Squar took the Boat (on her back)
and proceeded on to the Town 3 miles the
Day raw and cold wind from the NW"
(Captain Clark)

Clouds came in from the west.
Today a day of rain, wind and snow.
Small fingers and waves of clouds

gust into maelstroms.
They could blind, turn you around.
You could enter them one way and never

find the path out again, your footprints
erased by wind racing over land.
Land which is brown and spare.

Everything about it is a birthdate,
a woman's; she who has lost
her love but still lives with him.

Love from the Yellowstone Trail

1.

The historical society meets for a picnic tonight,
6:00 to 8:00, Senior Citizens Center, in a walnut-paneled room
off Highway 12. When the conversation tires
of <u>Barns Again!</u> it drifts on to Lewis and Clark.
What was eaten on the long trek. Venison. Bear. Bear
is good if you know how to fix it. Otherwise, it's all fat.
And bison. Little-known to known facts get spit out
over bowls of spaghetti salad, baked beans and dark chips—
which could be something Lewis and Clark took along,
now couldn't it?—You take a bison, so much easier
to raise than cattle. And bison like to slide around
on an iced-over pond. No. Yes! What about buffalo fish?
Big-headed monsters, though they're not local.
Carp are. The woman who lived in New York City once,
whose Navaho earrings swing when she turns her head,
saw carp for sale out there. It's a delicacy out East.
She asked the vendor where it was from and he told her,
"From a place you've probably never been in, far away,
in South Dakota." Big laugh out of that
from the historical society in faraway South Dakota.

2.

Of everything Valerian Three Irons has said
under the Chautauqua tent, my sister found
his talk on Sakakawea's name most interesting.
(Though she nodded off on her folding chair,
and more than once watched the hills around us,
where wind runs in tall grass, sleek and invisible
as guilt up the spine.) Sacagawea, Shoshone
for "boat launcher" ? Or Sakakawea—
the way the Hidatsas say it—"Bird Woman"?

22

She was thinking about Mr. Tobin, she whispers,
his mnemonic device so powerful its spell rises
sixty years later on a clear August morning.
She raises her hand to recite it.
"S-a, c-a, g-a, we-a." My sister says it again
for its rosary of comfort. "Sacagawea."

3.

A train goes by, a long chain of wheat cars
and coal cars labeled Burlington Northern.
My sister and I stand in the gravel road
beside the tracks, counting and waving
as if we were girls again. She, old enough
to have watched Hunkpapa and Hidatsa
dance in full dress at the depot for tips.

And now Lakota have moved in next door to her,
in the rented house. A soap opera kind of life.
The young woman pitches his clothes—jeans
and cowboy shirts—into the driveway, the back
door-bang punctuating each toss. Then he
catches her in an embrace, slowing down
the unconquerable with a kiss.

Two Voices from the Trail

1805

They don't see my lips moving when I answer their questions,
Charbonneau, Lewis and Clark. The answer's over and they haven't
caught it, the magpie, the voice of Three Sisters, the mother
ten thousand years old. Something marked but not bought,
spreading its velvet black tail with the convincing white streak.
A statement in shroud and revelation. Though they count my
hand when they vote in the encampment on the river, free-flowing,
narrow, swift in places. Lined by cottonwood groves. Water
for vast herds of game. Shelter for lodges with firewood at hand.
My son will become a Charbonneau with schooling. My daughter
stays at my side. At my dying when my sisters ask if they should call
my husband in, I'll shake my head. No. This last, quiet bed is mine.

2001

Under the thin blanket of the Milky Way and a starry
teapot, we pass the monument boosters built in the Twenties
to the only squaw worth living: She helped the white man.
Does she sense us? On the road to Bullhead with our car full
of family, the way the present moves across the prairie. History
stirs in ravines. Darkness covers box houses, school,
the trading post. We arrive at the encampment on Rock Creek,
where "The mosquitoes have been put to bed," or so the KLND
announcer says. The powwow begins. No beatings tonight
in Bullhead. No one high on koolaid laced with hairspray.
More dancers than watchers. When we drive back home,
a moon-struck windsail surfs the waves of a once great river.

Finding Sacajawea

This time 'round she's married a Lakota.
He stands beside his pick-up, its hood open.
She's on their deck with their little boy.

Sure, he says when I ask for directions.
Their girl hugs his leg, a position
children take when they aren't afraid

of their fathers. His shirt, the color
of a northern fall sky, ironed azure
blue, cotton caressing his shoulders.

This one's no Charbonneau.—Wind
in my ears now. I'm coasting downhill,
windows open, to a peninsula, to Sacajawea's grave,

the grasses flashing blue-yellow-green. Long about now
the woman's calling her little family in,
leading them to the table. "Food's on."

Braiding Three Reports to Make One Fact

That night at Fort Yates
when Sitting Bull turned himself in,
a night of clubbing and shooting—
Sitting Bull, lining up his sights
down the barrel of a gun,
ghost dance gun, ghost trigger, ghost
barrel, ghost bullets
killing four dog soldiers
paid to kill him, mortally
wounding two others—
when it was over
he lay in the dirt.
What happened is that
the one who betrayed him, the one
paid to ride into the fort as Standing Bear
rode out as sell-out Sam.
Sam retired like a white man
to a little house in Wakpala.

And I shall have some peace there,
for peace comes dropping slow . . .

Slow, as in sewn moccasins and carved peace pipes.
Sam hawked them on a blanket in town.
Dropping, like the grasshoppers that ate Sam's
rows of potatoes and chewed his straw hat.
"One big fellow even bit me on the shoulder!"
When Sam laughed, his eyes crinkled.
His evenings were full of the blackbird's wings.

Wounded Knee

What the eye holds, the heart holds, the ear holds.
Fourteen miles west of Philips, South Dakota,
on Interstate 90, I'm listening to W.A. Mozart,
a piece written in Salzburg, the Badland's baroque
coming up fast, *mako sica*'s pink architecture,
wind bridges and spires. Static making the music
ever more alien. I'm passing a herd of black angus,
Z Ranch Z's burned into hide. Whoever's
smelled a branding has an inkling of the air
near Auschwitz and Dachau, in Murnau
when the wind blew west. Burned flesh.
Singed hair. Such grief. Mozart would never.
His own set of inherited prejudices would be
ripped to the core: *How could honest Germans?*
Here the sky is so open it hides the stench of old massacres.

Dance Site on Standing Rock

Facing the warm south, the unnaming wind,
the site lies in a lea, a careful choice, the land's
own sheltered architecture. The skeletal

remains of sweat lodge and shade roof
circle a tree. Tied to its heart,
a bundle of grass. Scarves, knotted
in beads, dangle from its branches.

Dizzying to look up into the aspen,
then past it, into the sky, and learn
by foot, by skin, its slow, blue swirl.

Borders

*"(North and South Dakota) . . . were born
together; they are one, and I will make them
twins . . ."*
President Benjamin Harrison, 1889

From his desk in Washington,
he'll pencil an invisible line
through an infinity of grasses,
north-south, ignorant of
the land's natural division,

the flatter prairie flanking the river
on the east; on the west,
the way it rolls to mountains.

He'll ignore ancient warnings,
the story in <u>Judges</u>,
about cutting up one's daughter
to provide a stranger his lodging.

Directions will spill over
his borders as rose hips,
buffalo berries, chokecherries,
wild plum and the prickly pear.

Children will grow up warped, proud
to be from the south
or north of the same home.

So he should come, the President,
with his clocks and deeds,
pencils and imagination
between his legs and watch
the wind bury his borders in dirt.

The Wind

Her big sister phones to warn her a strong wind's blowing up out of the west. It should arrive tomorrow or the next day.

She leaves the house for one of those rare places, her back yard, to water trees. She hates lugging the hose around. It's his chore, but he's been gone four years, the last time the trees were watered. This fall, so hot and dry, she feels guilty at her seclusion inside the house.

All is quiet out in back. She hears a cricket. Then a robin; a flock is gathering. Under the amur maple she finds volunteers from the violet she planted in hopes it'd spread. For two? three? years she's missed this resurrection, one she's craved. And so to establish a neighborhood for violets only, she pulls up all the grass grown in wild among the wood chips.

It feels good, this controlling, shaping. Even so, she doubts her hands talk the same language as violets or grass. ". . . rode my Chevy to the levee . . . this will be the day that I die . . ." she hums and isn't afraid.

That afternoon the wind arrives and demolishes the hollyhock and its second harvest of white, lotus-like flowers floating in the air. The stalk collapses as if shot in the neck. Dastardly wind. Though she knows it's driven by no other motive than the four hundred miles it takes to get from there to here.

Another Love Letter

Irene Hartland, Dad. You could have had her by the looks of this photo.
Nice legs. Her silk stockings glare in the sun.
She's interested—standing beside you, curving in. The other girl
(my mother) on the left is too nice. Forget her. Irene is the one.
She likes your tender bulk in that winter coat with its fur epaulets.
She likes the sweater you wear underneath, and the way the collar
stands up like a prince's ruff around the back of your neck.
Consider her name, Dad. "Deer land." You'll be reasonably happy.
She's a German Russian, too, she understands how to handle men
like you.

No, not Irene? How about "Maggie?" Or Miss Fay? Or Miss Moon?
Tête a tête in the photo, your arm around her, you're bending down,
your six feet toward her, a wicked, sexy grin on your clean-shaven face.
Dad, stop right there. I'll go back to the universe and wait another round.
I herewith consign my sisters to the same, we slide gladly
out of the picture. For you.
For Vila Netz. Or the Billigmeier girl. Either of the Miller sisters.
They all have a crush on you, your sunglasses, round as quarters.
Remove us, your daughters, and you're a frat boy, a movie star,
advertiser, salesman, efficiency expert from 160 acres in North Dakota.

Look at you now!
You who would not listen. You are a big,
lumpy walrus, old, wearing a cap labeled *Sitting Bull Stampede*.
Smiling because you've found three women who can live with you
underwater for an hour at a time. Your arms slide easily around us,
your daughters, your girls. Where you've taped this photo
into the album, I find two of your gray hairs. Two from the grave?
I almost pull them out, and then realizing it's too late,
I let you be.

Haying

Summer's ebbing. Grasses wallow around the field tree
where the tractor's discs can't reach, where shade

thins and folds. Under the sun, the necessity
of a water bottle. Or at the century's turn, a jug, a brown

ceramic jug from Ukraine, seen in Soviet Realist paintings:
laughing farm hands on a mid-morning break: bread, radish,

and water, water the unmarried sister lugs out to the field,
its chaff and heat. The sun, at a zenith in a painter's blue sky.

This business is for horses, this discing, cutting, baling.
The field's and tractor's revolutions make good money

some years. Blunt and brusque, the tractor's blade
uncovers a world of slithering snakes, pheasant chicks,

red fox, and the grass's nomadic fragrances. It leaves
wakes of mown hay. Bales float to the horizon.

On the shore, the different world of house.
The tractor's the only ship on the Ocean with a Tree.

The Genealogist's Table

A tiny stage barely lit.
Dates, charts, bulky
as furniture
being shoved around.
Yellowed letters, snapshots
numbered
like beloved sand.
you like to know Wear We are Boarn?

And memory: a woman
firing a clay oven, feeding it
twisted slough hay,

children leading
a horse around a pole,
a dingy carrousel,
shaping the barn's dung
and straw into bricks for burning,

a man, following a trail
the Lakota made across the river.
The ice, like rubber.

Outside the window
the night hawk calls
from the creeks
Worthless and Rabbit.
amarca this countrey uncle Sam

Cream Puffs

Toward afternoon, snowfall ends on the farm.
Cold tests the walker, the woman who once mourned

the abdicated Kaiser, the lost Old World.
Leftover are the pleasures of her oven's pastry,

the cream separated from milk in the pantry,
something from the past her children can understand

and let melt on their tongues. Her resignation gathers
the way snow clusters on the windbreak's canopy

of snarls. At the country road she pauses, then turns
back home. Beyond the chimney's white column

lie the fields, a fence, a plow, the daily disguised
under snow as emblems from another world.

Old Glory Passes By

From a house on Standing Rock, lonely Highway 1806 south, the stars
and stripes flies straight over the rez, like the flag on the moon,
Great Sioux Reservation created, 1868

and across the bridge, a regiment of ranchers on horseback
struts Old Glory down Main past crowds of folks who remove their hats
Custer violates 1868 Treaty in Black Hills, 1874

and clasp their hands over their hearts while white-ankled palominos,
chestnuts, black stallions clop by, tails swishing, flanks shuddering,
Sioux must return to Reservation or be considered hostile, 1876

outpacing the floats, the rodeo princess candidates' and high school band's,
the class reunions' of '82 and '52, cluttered by brigades of small flags,
Teton Sioux win Battle of Rosebud, 1876

ditto the law firm's (Beitelspacher, Custer, Raabe & Red Hawk)
ignored by the young Lakota walking with his white girlfriend,
Lakota win Battle of Greasy Grass (Little Big Horn), 1876

teens holding hands through a gauntlet of averted eyes and
the curb's dust devils, dervishes of butts and dust, grit
Native lands established as Indian Territory, 1882

that gets in your eyes, and the eyes of the Lakota kids
drumming for the 21st Century Community Learning Center
Native American religious practices forbidden, 1883

where Bullhead's office name plate reads Mr. Bullhead.
I like the horseman who's undone his braids, let his hair
Reservations reduced in size, 1889

bloom thick and black over his bare, ample shoulders.
No trace on him of Old Glory's colors. Look:
    Ghost Dance Inaugurated on Pine Ridge, 1889

the Senate candidate's flaggy necktie and glory-gleam grin.
"No candy, no votes!" the voters half-joke, priming their kids
    Massacre at Wounded Knee, 1890

to hustle candy from Mr. Thune and the '57 Buick convertible
hawking the August Lewis and Clark Festival. I squirm
    Jim Thorpe (Wa-Tho-Huk) Olympic Champion, 1912

in the red-white-and blue matching socks and red USA T-shirt
my sister's bought for us to wear, Citizen Sister Twins.
    Lakota warriors serve in WWI

Behind heartbreaker cheer leaders—ten whites, two Lakota
(a better ratio than in my day: 12 to null)—the Golden Oldies
    American Indians become U.S. Citizens, 1924

on the Care Center float, harmonizing to Johnnie Olson
on his synthesizer, get drowned out by the city's fire trucks,
    Charles D. Curtis (part Kaw) elected Vice President, 1929

new and big-bucks yellow, a pair of wailing heroes
tossing sweaty kids more candy that rat-tats
    Lakota Code-Talkers serve under MacArthur, WWII

on the hot street like firecrackers under the Shriners'
swaggers, startling nobody when one falls off his go-cart.
    Occupation of Wounded Knee, February-May 1973

The scat crew, all shit-eating grin, brings up the rear, shoveling
piles of fresh horse apples perfuming lower Main. "That's it!"
  Leonard Peltier convicted of murder, 1975

We fold our chairs and go on home in time for the family picnic,
then sunset fireworks shooting over the Sitting Bull Stampede.
  Year of reconciliation between
  American Indians and non-Indians, 1992

House

"We went from house to wood.
For change in solitude."
—Robert Frost

About Houses (7 parts)

Go to your bosom. Knock there,
and ask what it doth know. <u>Measure for Measure</u>

1. Tea

Cold here in the aunt's living room.
Not enough money for heat. Over time
the cat shredded her green velvet drapes.

The air, once loving coffee's fragrance,
suffers from its long absence. Hell
is a wonderful spring day with no prospects.

Enter a robin. The first since winter began
its encampment, locking all rooms in
to their thin-walled selves. Then the bright,

orange call. O magic key.

2. Restless

This will have a happy ending. I want you
to keep reading through these walls—
you can smell everything, hear everything

osmosing papery divides. The curry odor
you hate, the canary next door, the love cries,
the genre-less music, every noise a bone

in the throat of privacy. But heaven's coming,
I don't know from which direction, but
just beyond the door I'm looking for.

I'm not the first who's wanted to believe this.

3. A Summer Voice Counsels the Use of Maps

There are worlds I know nothing about.
How is it I missed the little street called
Misery Before True Happiness?

Where was it? Before or after
the street I turned down?
I listen to the one who smiles,

I wouldn't change a thing in my life.
What street does she live on?
Which route did she take to get there?

Where did she get her map?

4. More on Walls

What if you were a woman in Darfur?
Raped on your way to the well and raped
again on the way back to your quarters,

a camp that reeks of outcasts and excrement,
a room, no, a tarp for a roof fastened to sticks
where you could say you live,

as in *I am dead in this hovel. But I exist.*
Your water vessel empty, maybe smashed.
You could pinpoint where fear comes from,

where it enters your thin walls.

5. Intermission

In a common area. Maybe near a plaza,
between its lions, Success and Near-success.
Between dusk and long day.

6. The Heart on the Corner

Is this a house with boarders?
Or a house with borders?
They change according to whoever

won the latest war. I speak
the language of the second story,
rubbery-walled chambers,

each with its own door and a voice
full of good will, yes, full, its
Come in, Come in, each morning

translating my desire.

7. Homecoming

So it isn't as if the heart were empty,
but that it's too full to see, too
busy with its lifting and falling,

attacks and seizures, swoons,
obstinate pulsing, violent eruptions,
its passions, knocking too fiercely

against the walls of its blunders.
A lopsided house,
a system of sluices and wonder.

All mine. All mine.

How Do We Live in Winter Without Zinnias?

It's flowerless unless you count ice
in crystals, more spoor than seed;
they do not perpetuate themselves.
Flower isn't as perfect a word as *summer*.
A summer, not as perfect as a zinnia.

Monday, from the elevator, I saw a woman

hunched over in her wheelchair, fallen asleep.
No. I'll think of the summer pot of flowers
awake on my table: zinnias, asters, gladiola,
straw and strawberry flowers, daisies
(white and lavender), and one rose dahlia.

Six Meditations on French Doors During a War

1. Paris

The house looked grave. As did the man
standing at his French doors. Then he washed
his hands of desire, over and under, his fingers,
a flurry in water. It was 1939, a year when nothing
came out but war. Despair advanced in small,
rectangular thoughts confined to a hand's cramped
movements across a wasted paper. Unrationed
light flooded through the door, swirled over
the floor's flatland, wetting the man's polished
shoes in shiny puddling. When he recalled
the First, the Great War, the rabbit's foot
in his pocket felt more dead than lucky.
Outside lilacs, withering sirens, bloomed.
Les lilas étaient en fleur, a sound he would later
consider a most beautiful sentence, even in German.

2. The Prairie

He saw the house first as wrecking site,
walked past it every day for a week
on his way home from the plant, watched
the house fall, board by board, heard
the screams nails make under a crow bar.
He sucked in a gasp: all that good
wood going for scrap.

                         He was willing
to haul the door on his back three blocks home.
Got it for next to nothing, something his wife
could close and still see through. Its key,
long and skeletal and crusty, still in the lock hole.
The luscious, final consonants—Fre*nch*—stuck
between his full lips and her tongue's hot well.

45

3. Her Side

Light, slightly hung yellow, slow and somnolent,
fell through her new French door, ah!
A door that lived because a quarrel ended
with a gift, something that said, *I'm sorry.*
When a chinook blew in from the West—air, air!—
she opened her heart like her French door.
That there was only one, she overlooked.
A split heart in '39 could be overlooked.
Half-measures in '39 could be overlooked.
Though on dusting days, the housewifey battle
taken pane by pane, she nailed a list of complaints
to the glass like Luther's thesis to the church door.
You love straggler for glamour.
You half-wit in a humble pie of a house.
You elegant one-winged opening and closing.

4. Unless You Are Superstitious . . .

it's only a draft
in the house, shaking
the French door,
it isn't the door's
assent, or rattled
differing opinion
expressed over
a cup of tea.
You might wonder
at this door, how its
frankness is ignored—
open, it looks shy; closed,
open—its nature shouts
the wars inside a room
through its glass skin.

5. A History Behind One Door

Because she was so nervous, she lost
the twenty dollars her mother slipped
into her pocket on her wedding day.

She never found it. If there
was a god, he didn't do her
any favors then. It was

that kind of war, revealing
more of herself
than she'd see in the glass

French door, a constant in the house,
like stars over the roof but
so much more. Tangible. Once

she'd been a bride and her groom
cut plum blossoms
down by the river for their wedding.

6. Peace

The desire not to be hurt but touched,
yes, every French door wants that,
wants, perhaps, a more significant path,
less limited to the breadth of its swing.
Still, its path is stately, and its name,

melded with the fragrance of lilacs,
isn't too presumptuous. Except
to the free-roving moon whose light
enters the room through glass panes,
presses itself on the door's brass handle.

Sometimes, when the door is half open,
it wrestles with its shadow, how to stand
close and be connected with the missing
half, that would be Heaven, the door's
tongue at rest in another's Edenic catch.

Three on Hell

All over town dogs bark *water water.*
Their masters are at work
on Sunday morning hangovers.

Dog chains beat paths into the heat.
A husky rubs his misery against
one old tire left out for him.

He scrapes his fur down to bare.
A shadow puddles near.
Water! Water!

*

Tumbleweeds claw the fence.
The goatsbeard I saw struggling
to bloom, I named Brave Seed.
Ignorant young toads that left
a leaf's shade, roast on sidewalks.
Houses stand cowed by paper-thin shade.

*

"Depression-like drought,"
my sister whispers beside me,
"hate to see my water bill."
An old couple wanders down Main,
wading the street's shimmering mirage.
On the Christian Thrift Store's mural
Jesus bargains, offering life
to the Samaritan woman
in exchange for water from her well.

Dress Shoes

As far as the shoestrings go,
if you could breathe on them,
they'd turn to smoke.
But you cannot. They're out of reach.
Six-foot-under in the coffin, laced
the old-fashioned way, parallel
to each hole, not crossed over the tongue.
A leather lodge for the foot's own arch.

A foot once so heavy it was very much
the metaphor for a bloated word
like "ache," but now it fits
the paradox of leading in while lying
still, a light airy being,
in a pair of windowless rooms.

Bees

those old men on motorcycles
cross sunlit Saharas, the blossoms'
petals, serious attachments

buzzing

intense affairs with the biggest and boldest,
the pale, northern hibiscus called hollyhock,
the red threads in a peony's mound,
the yucca's white bells, hanging silent

buzzing

what a whisper
could never be—ponderous,
voluminous bulge and pulse,
Russian fragility

buzzing

their summery
eponymous natter
between fuse and hummer.

Teleportation

Back then men in the family smoked in the living room while the women did up the dishes in the kitchen. After a Sunday morning sermon based on Habakkuk's prophesies, the sitters let their minds wander into their own future. Would anyone of them live till the year 2000? One uncle predicted a someday-machine that'll wash clothes automatically. "It's already here," someone yelled, slapping his knee. "Ja, and power steering, too." Another said he couldn't drive without it.

Fixing Potato Salad While the Past Comes and Goes

Mid-August morning at the kitchen counter.
    Potatoes and eggs, already boiled.
        My mother peeled them hot.

And her mother and now me. Oh, it looks so easy.
    The garden's 260 pound harvest carried in
        to the kitchen, cooked up. One day at a time.

Windows open. Cool breeze. Somewhere down the street
    a kid, cranky, hot, bored, crying.
        I'll give you a whop.

Food. A family history of it. Who cut the roast,
    who baked, who tried to escape clean-up,
    who rolled in the grass after eating too much,
    who buttered his refrigerator cookies,
    who crashed to the floor in a farmers' cafe,
    sausage half chewed in his mouth,
    who made something out of nothing,
    who had only milk and flour when a child,
    in whose house was light craved more than food.

All this in my hands. I mix up the dressing.
    Core the green pepper. Dice red onion.
        Did any of them know red onion?

They planted yellow, white and spring green onions,
    their gardens' delicacy. One ghost cautions
        over my shoulder, "Easy on the onion."

The one who didn't like onion. Hated garlic.
    Loved Italian pasta. Go figure. Easy. Easy.
        Not too heavy-handed.

The kitchen spins as it does when sun breaks though clouds
    and light expands the room into world. Then cloud
        cover returns, and I'm looking at a plain, round bowl.

Of the Little Store Near the Park, the Best

and worst of it that could be said is, it survived the war, like war its supplies consistently dwindling. Ask for laundry soap, and Mrs. B. hurried away through the curtains behind the counter to fetch it, her broad back all hustle, her hair black, curled and neat, her flowery homemade dress, pretty. Once in a while Mr. B., pale and unsteady, rang up a sale.

The Bs' grocery had no truck with aisles,

and if it did aspire to them, the ambition never was fulfilled. Wall shelves supported a soldier-ly line-up of cans: Spaghettio, Spam, Dinty Moore Beef Stew and a brigade of piggy-colored fat kids hawking Campbell's soup. Bread had its own stand, the Wonder Bread stand, movable as a clotheshorse and as sparse, for most women in that town baked their own bread.

So there was no wandering through the store,

only abrupt directness, face-to-can encounters, hand-to-wrapper, the eye forced to fall to the lowest shelf to assess the meager cache of candy, or on Sundays, a plump and belted stack of newspapers near the door. I searched the comics for the rare appearance of paper-doll panels, three cute outfits for a girl with black curly hair, whose name I'll recall some night in a dream.

You could say the little store was a giant

pantry or a public closet with a deep box freezer, in itself a kind of cavern in an otherwise above-board town, a frosty grave for sweets sold by the pint or popsicle. But the Bs' brand of scarcity never triumphed over a world of abundance. It made the store freakish and miraculous at the same time, like everyone, dying even as it lived, a bit at a time, a rare character oddly here and then—

after Mr. B. first, and then Mrs. B.—gone.

Spider Webs

The complications of sheer threads in sunlight,
woven bonds around this desolate house,

possession's song in the eaves, in the well's
roof, the shed, the trees' crooks, the rusted vise

mounted on the clothesline pole. Still,
no one marches around, waving a broom.

Who's interested now in being fastidious?
The wind? It's never wind's intention,

though always within its direction, to sweep,
hassle, topple whatever isn't firmly fixed.

And wind calls this house home every day.
So who can understand what is flimsy,

how a web perseveres. No, grows
and takes over, locking out departures.

Only simple physics remains:
You have left and now are gone.

Ring

What if an object, say a ring, prayed daily,
the mantra a ring hums to change
its location? For a ring, gracing
a softer, more leisurely hand.

Say then that this ring, a wedding ring,
was misplaced in a rain coat pocket.
The husband was yelling, the woman
looking high and low. "Maybe it went

down the drain." The marriage did.
Goodwill got the coat. A secretary
bought it, liking the padded shoulders.
She slipped it on like good fortune,

hopped the train west to Missoula.
Imagine her surprise one cool day,
while walking to work at Al's Motors,
to find a ring in her pocket. It looked

pretty bouncing along on her finger
as she typed or read a romance at lunch,
herself, the clever, frugal woman providing
her own gold ring if ever a *he* proposed.

The Pillow Cleaners Come to Town

and turn the senior citizen center
into an automated assembly line.

Goodbye, dross of long winter nights.
Farewell, old skin cells and reek:

what couldn't come clean on a clothesline.
Bundles of pillows, caroming, bouncing,

sloshing along, even as more
mistresses of pillows hurry through the door,

hugging stained sacks of feathers
as if they were thoughts and old defects—

oh, we paid so dearly for them—
but kept well past prime.

Bed

This is how it is between them.
He is cold. He lies wrapped
in flannel sheets, wool and
electric blanket, the best
gift she's ever given him.

She sprawls on her side,
warm to hot, throwing
off the top sheet, in the dark
longing for the love
she once thought was very cool.

West River Wedding
for Teresa and Casey

She goes out into her lover's fields,
cuts wild flowers for their wedding table,
for corsages, her bouquet, for the altar.

Armfuls of sunflowers and medicine dock,
mauve coneflower, blazing stars, prairie
onion and, for their rich, nutty-brown

and chartreuse green, nettles, too.
There's enough left over for their trailer.
She sews her wedding dress there.

Later she'll finish her degree in nursing,
But first, she'll dance so hard at her wedding,
the hall will spin itself from happy to silly.

Clean-up will be easy: open the hall's
back door and toss the flowers to the wind,
to the four corners of Corson County.

Their tumbling will stop eventually—
caught by barbed wire
or weighed down by snow.

Earth will take the splintered stems in.
Birds will eat the seeds.
Wild fire will use the rest for kindling.

The Wedding Feast

The pork roast is succulent, courtesy
of the local pig farmers association,
accompanied by corn on the cob
and one hundred pounds of spuds
fixed au gratin. Prepared and served
by retirees, bent by their bending; well
accustomed to stoves, they pick up
small change doing the hall's weddings.
For dessert, angel food. Pink angel food.
The bride, with high forehead and flying veil,
kisses a speck of frosting off the groom's
nose. He likes to be licked, you can tell.

With dessert, a slide presentation: photos
of the clean-cut groom we thought we knew
slumped, sozzled and lusty, birding the camera.
"Naughty," his grandmother whispers.
"Who put this together?" his father demands.
The cash bar stays open. By and by, the hall
lists into a starry heaven, gossamer veils
strung with tiny lights, a once upon a kingdom
guarded by sputtering candles and bubbles,
its paths pebbled with pink and blue M&Ms.
Children hop in delight, little shenanigans
resembling the future fall asleep in their mothers' arms.

The Old Made New

Who has set out this feast? A smorgasbord
from north of the Mediterranean. I'm hungry—
but something simple, please, something
common, the bread from this morning.

Who's walked through which market selecting
salmon over eel, tongue over thigh, the herring's
dead gaze over the trout's, fine olives from Provence
over those which blackened near the Parthenon?

Someone's found delicacy in the slaughterer's
hands, showing off the work on finest plates,
thick clay, Tuscan sun yellow, each rim chilled
by a sprig of parsley. Someone's included a sweet,

white onion to clear my palette. In a dream
the dreamer is both subject and object. Which part
of me prepared and spread this out like wonder?
Eat, eat, it demands and waits to see my first choice—

mine to arrange on my plate. Blushing rose
beside solid black, a gray quieting blood-brown.
On a clothed table, *en plein air,* comforting all. Take,
eat. Salmon. Herring. Olives. New tongue.

Two Sisters at the Breakfast Table

The older is busy inside her head
trying to connect
with the mourning dove down the alley.
The other is laughing at her, sitting there
coo-wooing over a bowl of Cheerios.

Hers is a wavering, wobbly coo,
a coo in search of a nest,
a coo invulnerable to whatever
lies in the way of getting
a bird call right. Her lips,

puckered, regimented
by a ring of wrinkles.
The voice, as intense as a wish
that the real bird, and only
that bird, return her call.

Like a Train Going By

In the quiet in the moment,
before sleep, on its edge,
I can hear time passing by
in some warp, holding us.

Before sleep, on its edge,
my father who is dead tells me,
"I can hear time passing by."
He and his parents ride in it.

My father who is dead tells me,
"Tonight I didn't eat so much."
He and his parents ride on it,
in sleep, on an empty stomach.

Tonight I didn't eat so much.
Now we have a chance.
He and his parents ride in it,
in some warp holding us.

Now we have a chance
to cure ourselves with medicine,
in some warp holding us,
with healing proverbs and old wine.

To cure ourselves with medicine,
we close the doors against evening.
In some warp holding us
at the same age; its noise is time.

We sleep better together,
in the quiet in the moment.
In some warp holding us,
I can hear time passing by.

Acknowledgments

Many thanks to the following magazines for publishing the following poems or their variations:

"First Baptist Church," "Variations on Water," "Like a Train Going By": *The Notre Dame Review*

"(Upper Missouri:) Fire and Water," "Another Love Letter": *Water~Stone Review*

"The Preacher on Daniel and Ezekiel": *Hudson Review*

"Three on Water," "Borders": *Blue Earth Review*

"The River's Arguments," "How Do We Live in Winter Without Zinnias": *Great River Review*

"River Woman": *Louisiana Literature*

"Notes from the (Lewis and Clark)Trail," "(The Missouri and its Headwaters) First a River," "Haying": *Ascent*

"'10th November, Satturday 1804'": *Full Circle* (online)

"West River Wedding": *Dust and Fire*

"The Wedding Feast": *Blueroad*

"Braiding Three Reports to Make One Fact": *Whistling Shade*

"Dress Shoes": *Blue Mesa Review*

"The Old Made New": *Flyway*

"Two Voices from the Trail," "Love (Letters) from the Yellowstone Trail": *Ontario Review*

"Six Meditations on a French Door": *Kalliope*

"Dance Site": *Pirene's Fountain* (online)

"The Pillow Cleaners Come to Town": *Talking Stick*

"Old Glory Passes By": *North Dakota Quarterly*

I'm also very grateful to poet colleagues and friends who've critiqued my work patiently and with keen eyes over the years.